DEPRESSION

The Way In. The Way Out.

Simon Robinson

DEPRESSION: THE WAY IN. THE WAY OUT.

This edition is a substantially revised and expanded work,
distinct in structure, content, and presentation from earlier editions
previously published under the same title.

Revised edition published 2025

ISBN (Paperback): 978-1-0684310-3-6

Simon Robinson
www.drsimonrobinson.com

Printed and distributed by IngramSpark
Printed in Australia, UK and USA

READER NOTICE:

This book reflects personal experience and interpretation.
It is not medical advice and does not replace professional care.

If you are feeling unsafe, overwhelmed, or at risk of harming yourself, please seek immediate support from a healthcare professional or a trusted local crisis service.

This book does not ask you to move faster than you can.
Nothing here requires agreement, belief, or endurance.

If at any point the material feels like too much,
stopping is part of the work.

Chapter 1

I notice how hard it is to say what this is.

Even living inside it, the shape keeps slipping away.

Every word feels either too heavy or too thin, as if the thing itself refuses a proper outline.

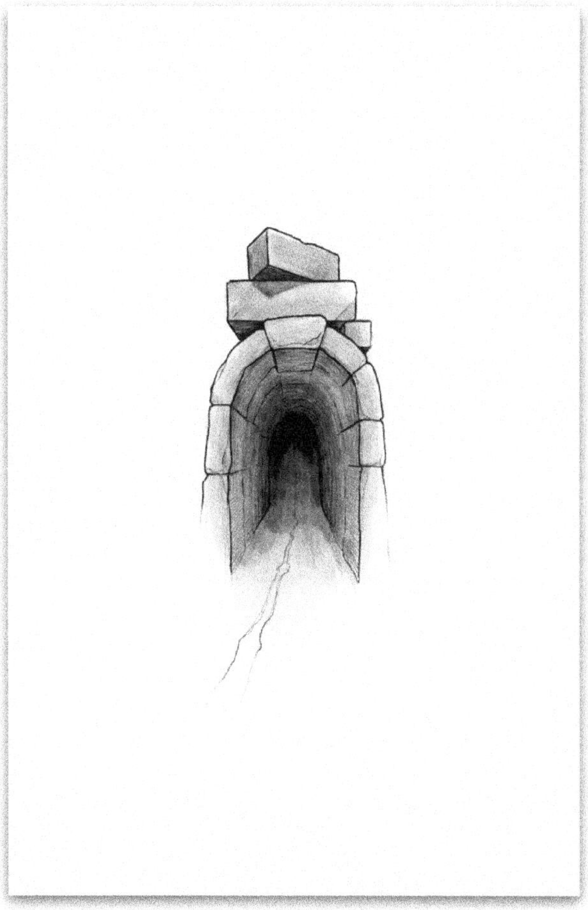

The first signs do not arrive as certainty.
They come sideways—through questions, pauses,
glances that linger a little too long.
I recognise myself being seen before I recognise anything myself.

I know the language for this.

I have used it for others.

Yet when it turns inward,

the words no longer organise what is happening.

I learned how to hold things in.

It was noticed. It was praised.

Over time, it stopped feeling like a choice

and started feeling like a role.

I kept moving.

Tasks were completed. Conversations answered.

Somewhere inside, nothing was reachable anymore.

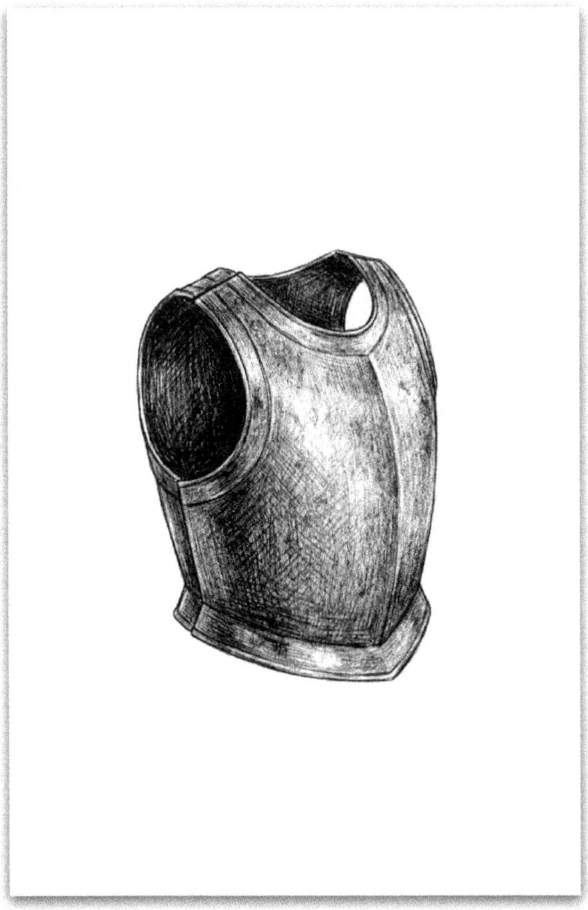

Each time something was swallowed, it stayed.

Not loudly—just added to the weight.

Over time, everything felt denser, harder to move.

I became reliable.

People leaned, and I did not move.

The admiration felt distant, and I stood alone with it.

The days flattened.

Nothing felt quite real, and admitting that felt worse.

I learned new ways to conceal what was already empty.

There were things that helped, briefly.

The relief faded, and the cause remained.

I returned again, not convinced, just hoping.

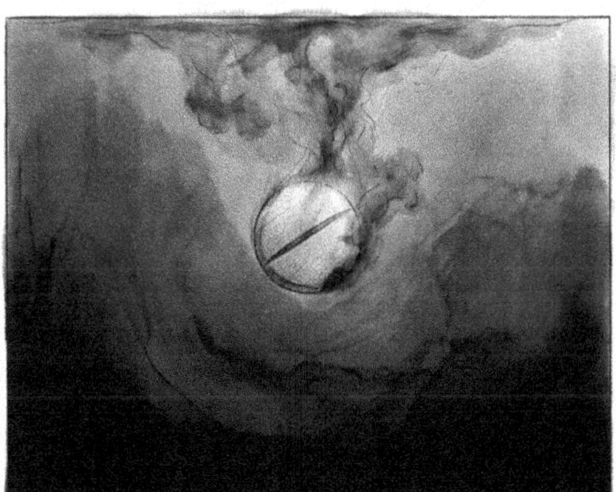

Eventually the distance would not hold.

Structures loosened. Days blurred together.

I began to disappear from the edges inward.

There were moments when I wanted it to stop.

Not life, exactly—just the pressure of being inside this self.

It felt like desperation, not decision.

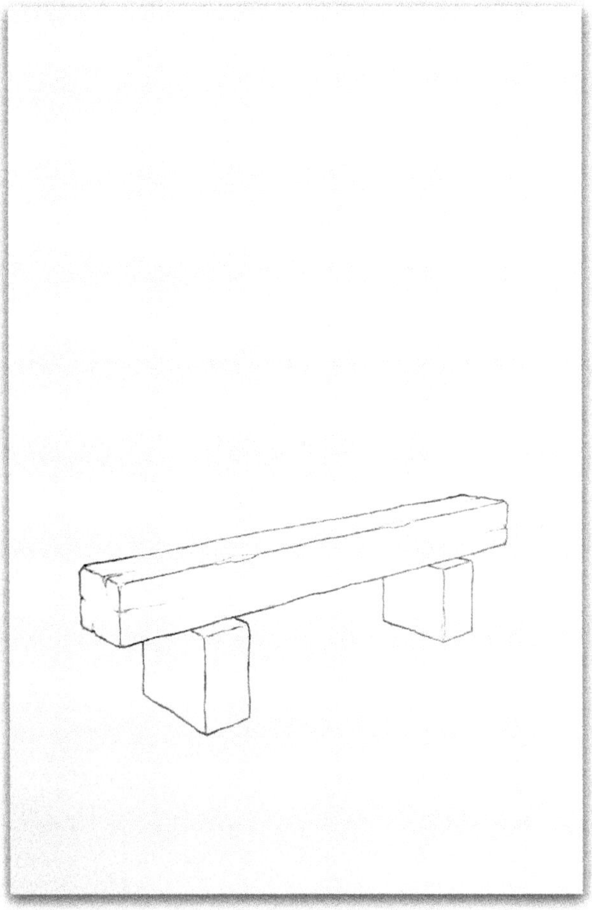

I did not find a cure here.

Only the sense that a way exists, slowly, quietly.

Enough presence to remain and to point.

Chapter 2

I learned the atmosphere before I learned language.

Which faces softened. Which tightened.

What made me closer, and what made me drift away.

Things sorted themselves quickly.

Good felt safer. Bad felt smaller.

I did not question the system. I used it.

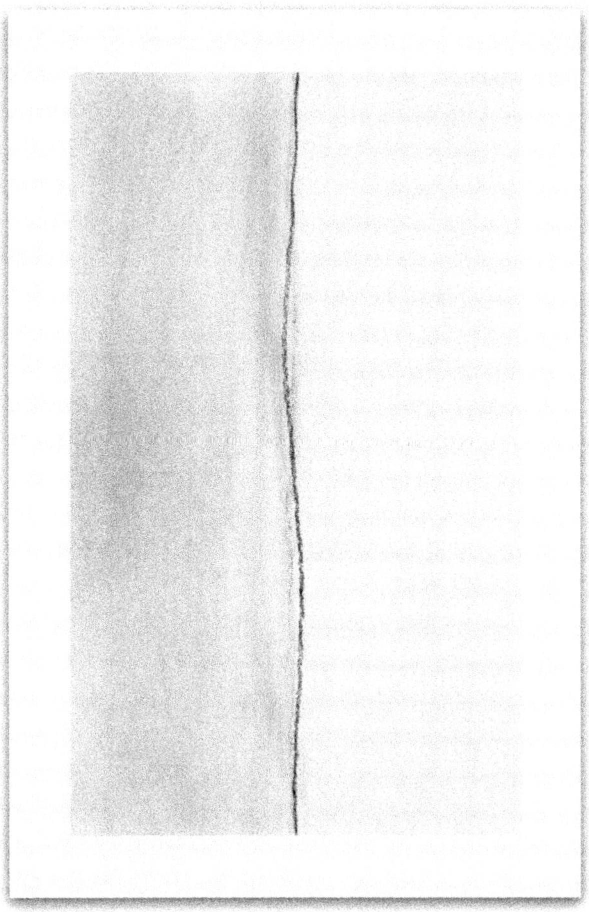

I watched what was done, not just what was said.

When I copied it, the rules changed.

The reason was never explained.

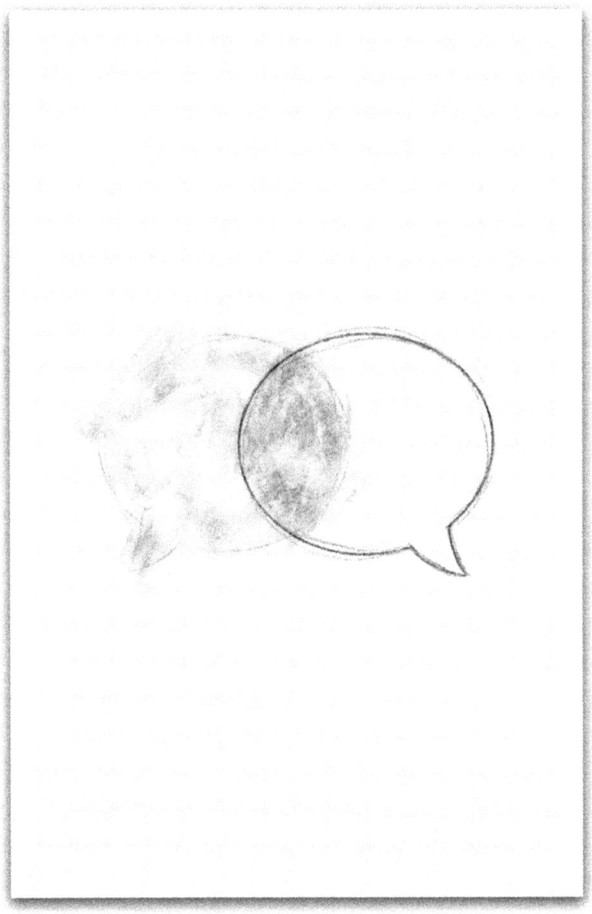

I asked the same thing in different ways.

Not for comfort, but for a verdict.

I wanted to know if I was allowed to stay.

When the label stuck, something else followed.

Distance.

After that, rebellion felt less like choice and more like gravity.

Belonging did not feel optional.

Being pushed out felt physical, not symbolic.

My body understood before I did.

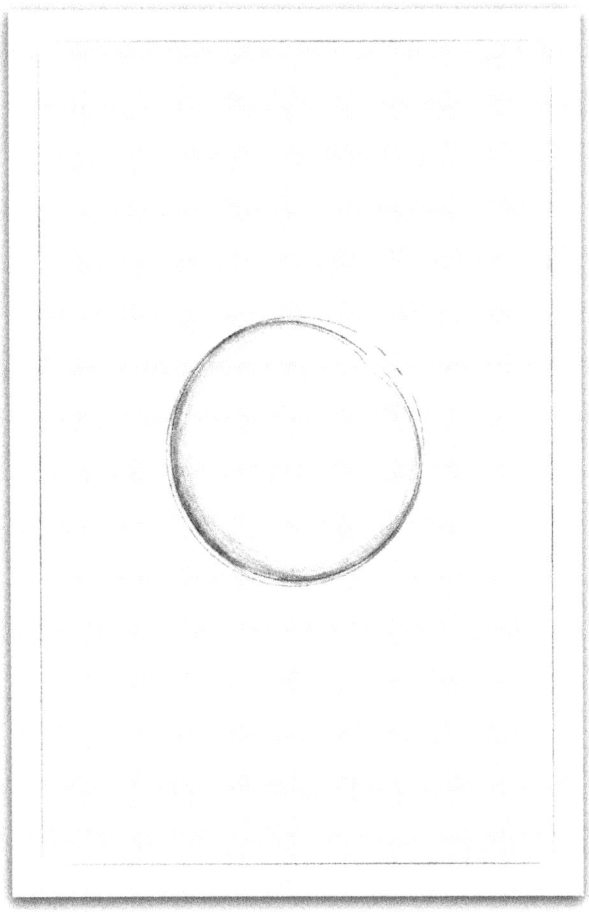

I learned what to show.

What stayed hidden did not disappear.

It learned how to wait.

Sensitivity became something to manage.

Fear became something to erase.

The lesson was quiet, and it stayed.

I was praised for coping.

I took the praise seriously.

Over time, numbness felt like progress.

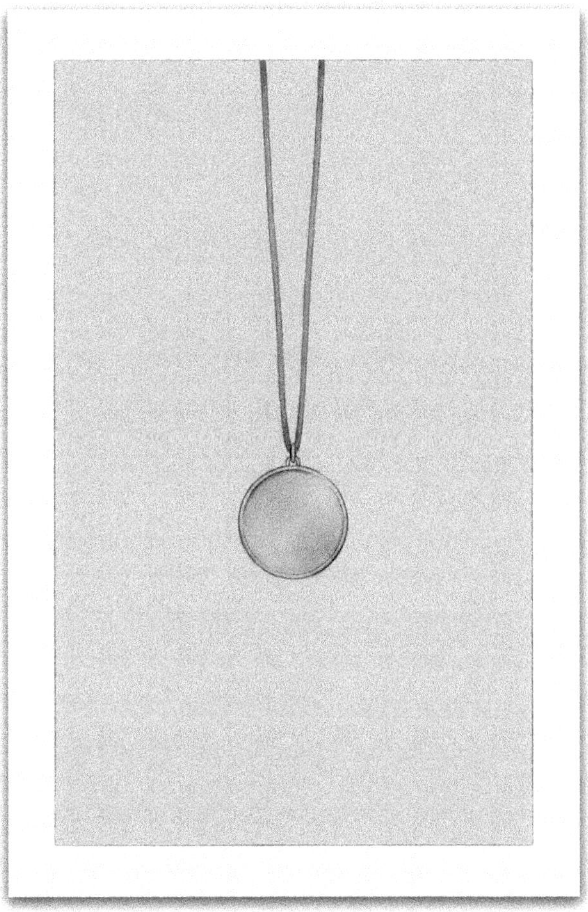

Years passed quickly.

Responsibilities stacked neatly.

What I felt never quite arrived in time.

The dullness became harder to tolerate.

I reached outward for anything that cut through.

The reach itself felt restless, not chosen.

What once protected me began to weigh me down.

I could not name the problem.

Only its mass.

Chapter 3

Life kept going.

I did what needed doing.

Nothing arrived to meet me inside it.

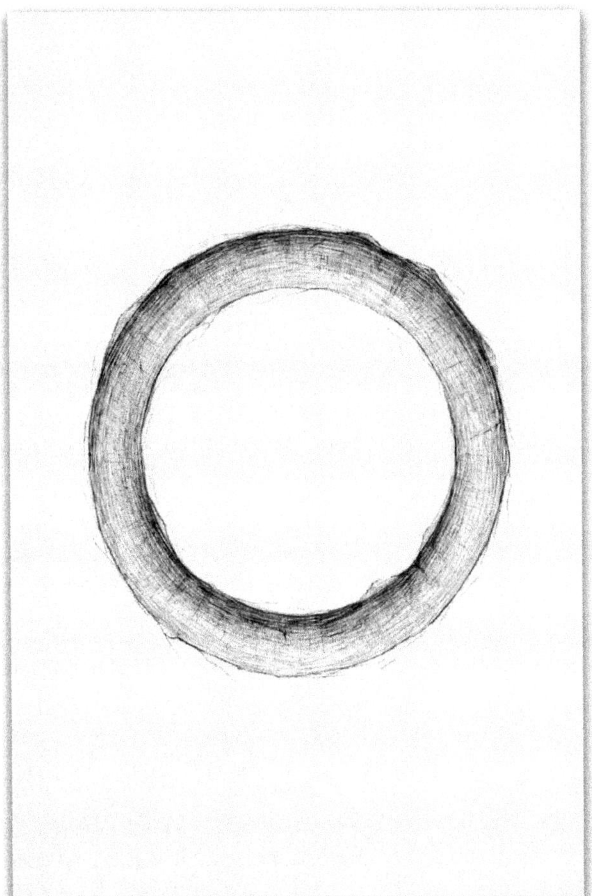

Small things began to cost more.

Not in minutes, but in weight.

What used to happen on its own required force.

I was not sad.

I was not anything in particular.

The blankness felt louder than sorrow.

Other people looked worried.

I wasn't convinced.

I went anyway, as if agreeing to a formality.

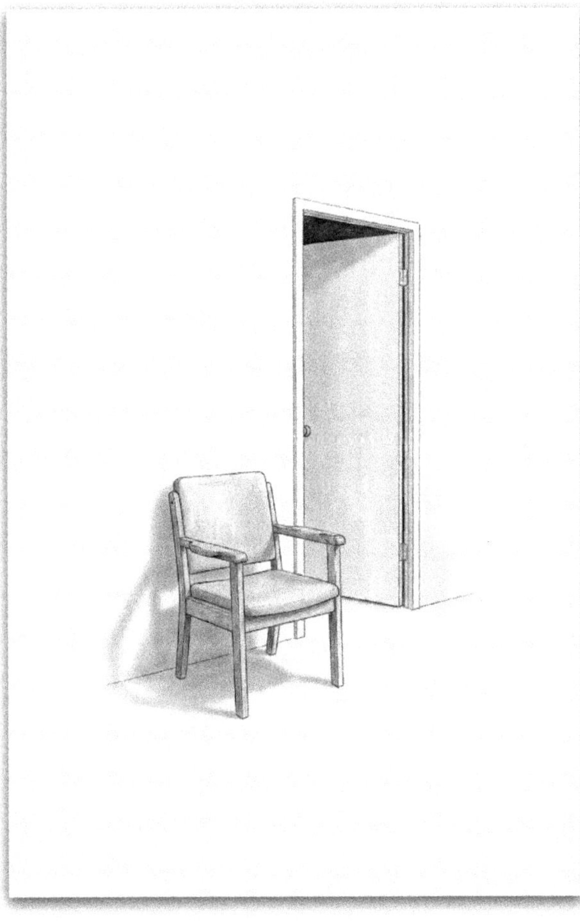

I kept holding.

People leaned, and I stayed upright.

I did not know how to put the weight down.

I began asking what life meant.

Not out of philosophy.

Out of distance—because nothing felt close anymore.

I missed who I used to be.

I couldn't name the moment I lost them.

Only the absence where they had been.

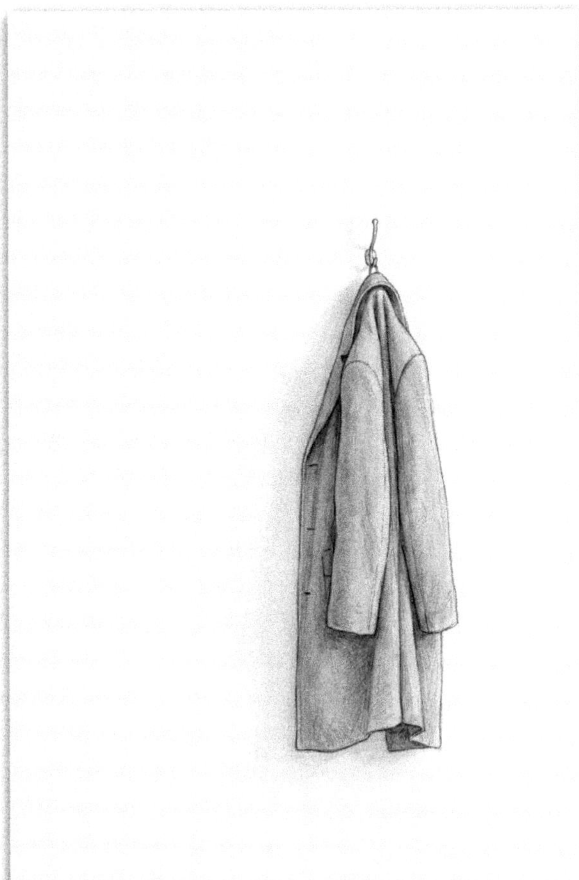

Coping had become my definition.

Letting it go felt like erasure.

So I tightened it, even when it hurt.

A new sensation appeared.

Not sadness—something sharper.

A fear that I might feel too much, too fast.

Other people's lightness began to sting.

I felt irritation flare without warning.

It left me ashamed, and then empty again.

My inner speech turned colder.

I rewrote my own history in darker ink.

Even good memories felt suspect.

I withdrew.

The room became smaller around me.

Care began to feel undeserved, like an error.

There were moments I wanted an end to the strain.

Not a plan—just a wish for silence.

Something in me felt thinned, as if coming apart at the seams.

Chapter 4

Something had been happening beneath my language.

Beneath my choices.

I lived on the surface of myself, and called it the whole.

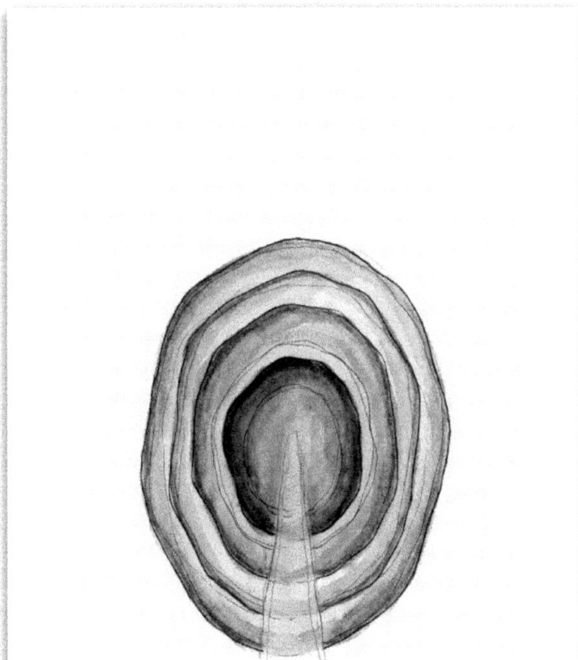

The weight arrived first.

Only later did I suspect it was feeling, compressed into density.

Not a message anymore—just a barrier.

It felt like passing through one threshold into another.

Not chosen. Not announced.

Habit became a downward motion.

Relief was taken where it was easiest to take it.

The relief never stayed.

Shame followed, and the world became smaller.

There were times I wanted an end to the strain.

Not action—just cessation.

A long, dim waiting without colour.

At some point I realised the old name no longer fit.

That recognition was brutal.

And then, oddly, it loosened something.

ID CARD

Roles stopped holding.

The inner reference point went missing.

There was no centre—only functions continuing.

Small things began to ignite me.

The heat arrived before thought.

Innocence in others started to feel like accusation.

Life stayed close.

Warmth reached the edge and stopped.

Love became sound behind a wall.

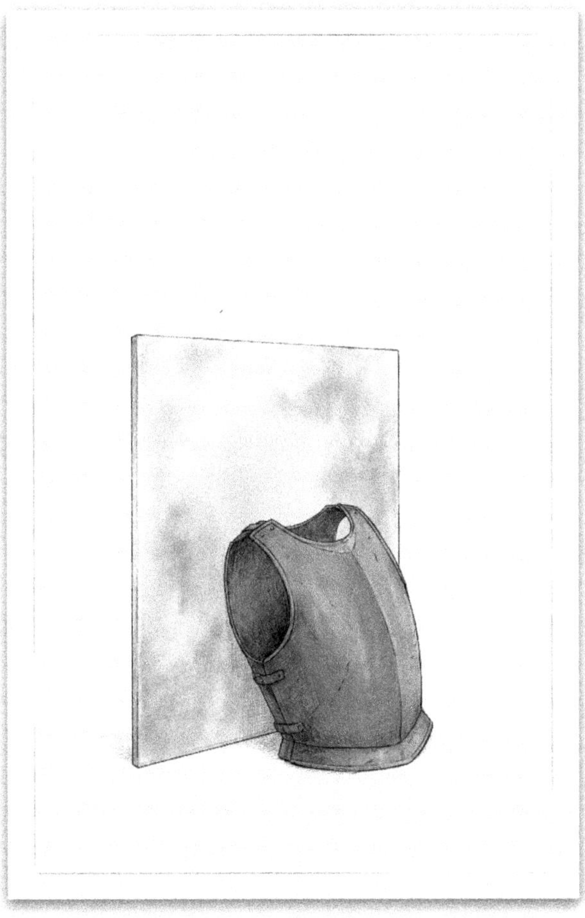

It began to feel as if something else lived inside me.

Not a monster—older skins, still moving.

Hollow layers carrying residue.

Mistrust started quietly.

A thin whisper at the edge of thought.

Interpretation became reflex before contact.

When feeling went missing, rules stepped in.

The mind compensated with categories.

The world became wrong-shaped and unforgiving.

Anger stopped being about one thing.

It became a weather system.

Desolation made every memory taste the same.

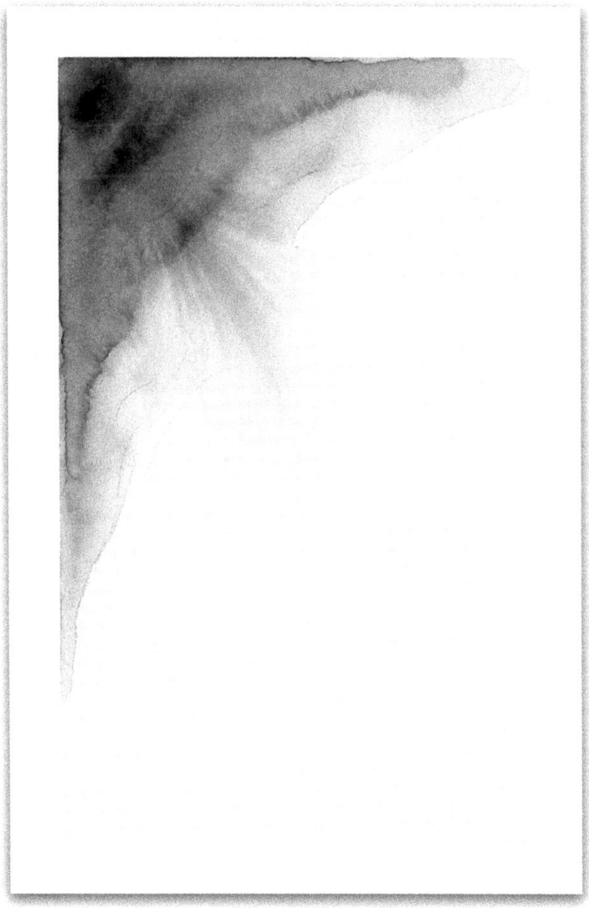

At the deepest layer, motion ceased.

Thought became a maze with two voices arguing in the dark.

Not revelation—just fragmentation and drift.

Chapter 5

What once looked like coping became distance.

The rewards arrived, and so did the wall.

I kept functioning, and quietly stopped living.

My interpretations changed first.

The world looked wrong-shaped, suspicious, dim.

As if the lens were smeared from inside.

There were moments I wanted the torment to stop.

Not a plan—only a craving for an end to this version of me.

A door in the mind that did not open.

Something broke that I had relied on without naming.

The ground I stood on no longer held.

I could not summon the old confidence by will.

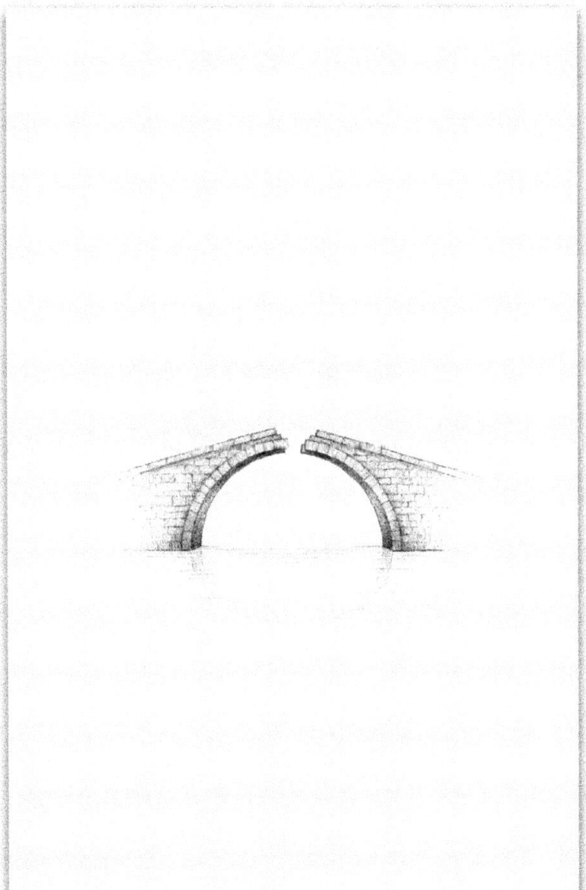

The old personality did not return.

It thinned under pressure and doubt.

I saw, with grief, that there was no return.

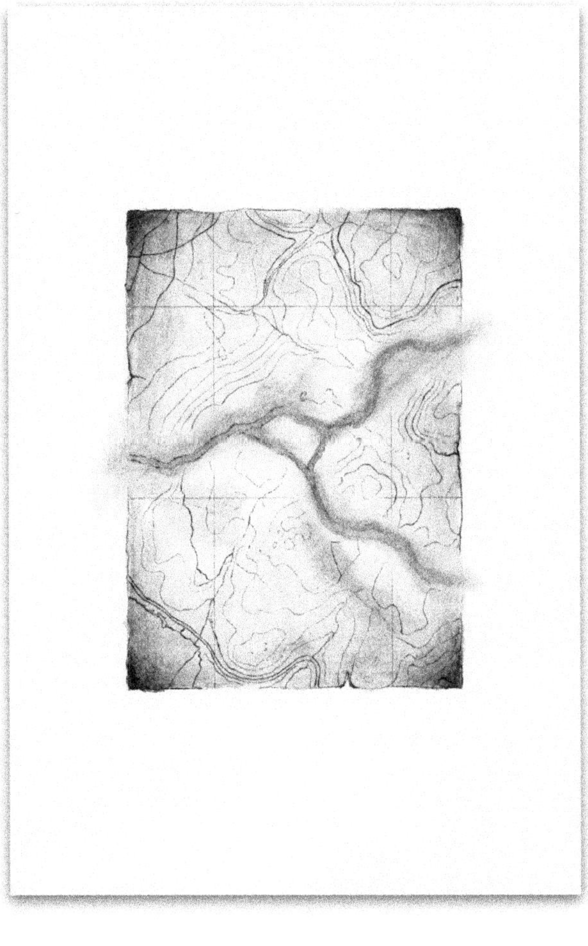

I missed the time before questioning.

Not nostalgia—more like missing an unbroken line.

The simplicity I once inhabited without noticing.

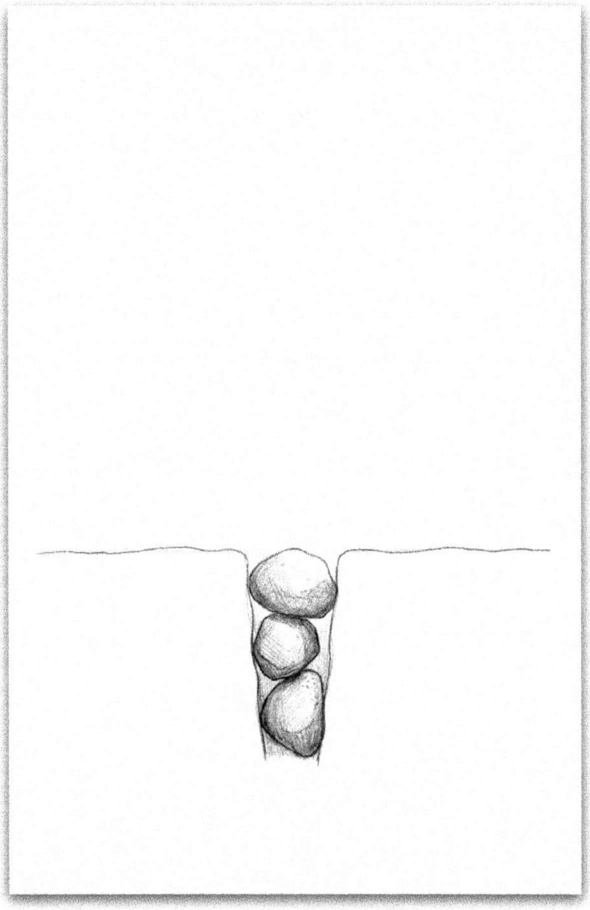

Time began to feel altered.

The inner world echoed, thin and distant.

I lived in a between-place without a name.

Doubt arrived like severing.

Not argument—removal.

One by one, the old supports fell away.

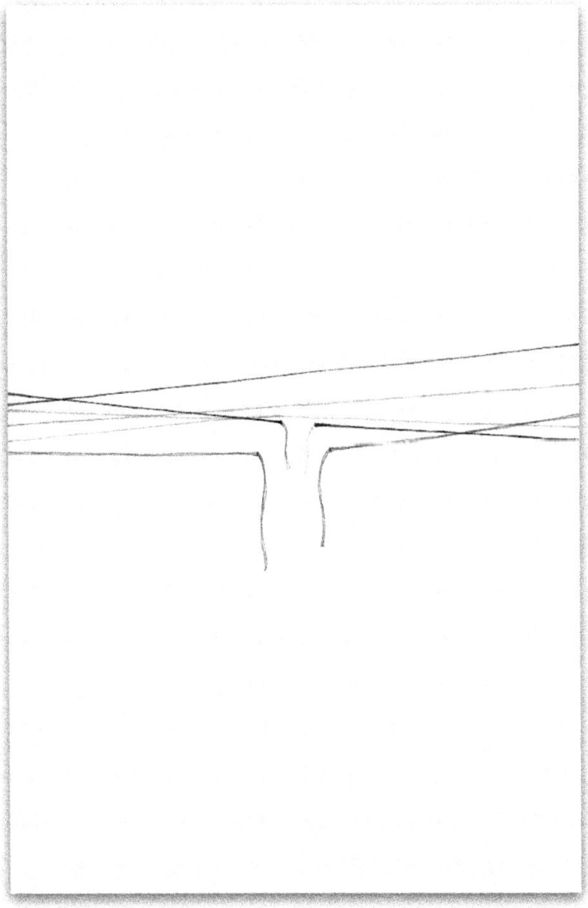

I was alone in a way that wasn't solved by company.

Even comfort felt unbelievable.

As if no witness could reach me there.

Eventually the struggle ran out.

Not triumph—exhaustion.

The self stopped trying to hold itself together.

The night did not end.

But it became quieter.

Less fighting, more stillness inside the same dark.

Hope arrived without my help.

Small, foreign, unmistakable.

Not warmth yet—just a thin line of real.

Something began, quietly.

Not confidence—more like possibility.

A small life under the old weight.

I wasn't healed.

Only past the worst point of pressure.

Everything needed to be simpler, slower, safer.

Chapter 6

The worst point had passed.

I was not well, but I was no longer falling.

The landscape stayed hard, yet it felt different.

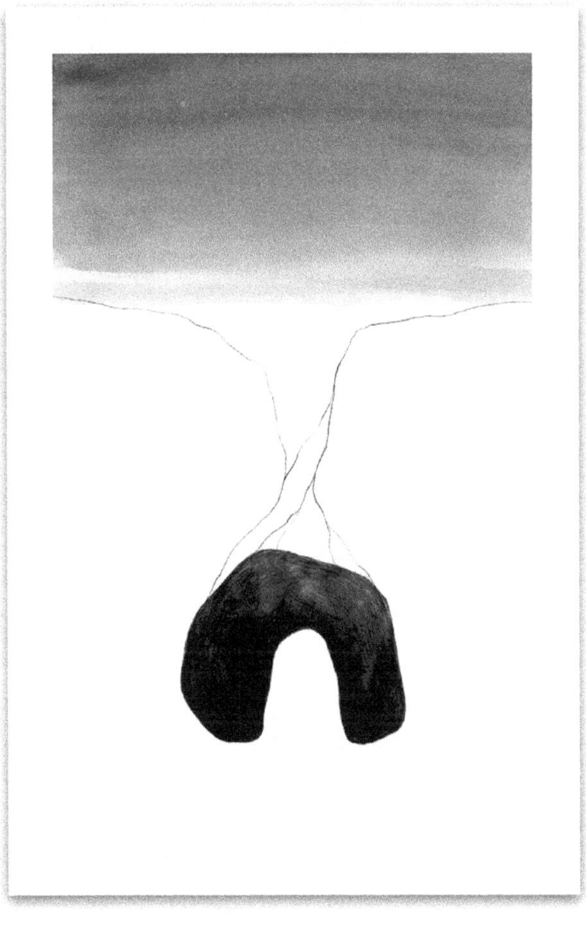

Everything looked the same.

The same rooms, the same tasks.

But it didn't land the same inside me.

Something small felt real.

Not strong enough to name.

Only strong enough to protect.

Warmth existed.

It reached me warped, as if through residue.

The distortion felt personal, but it wasn't chosen.

I kept it quiet.

I stayed vague on purpose.

I let it remain unqualified, like something newly planted.

I went down through the layers.

I listened.

I stopped when it was enough for that day.

I felt protective of the one who suffered.

As if they were someone I had been too harsh with.

A tenderness I didn't expect began to appear.

I noticed the small whispers.

The pessimism, the quiet distortions.

Seeing them did not require punishment.

Finding the stain felt like good news.

It meant it was not the whole cloth.

It meant something could lift.

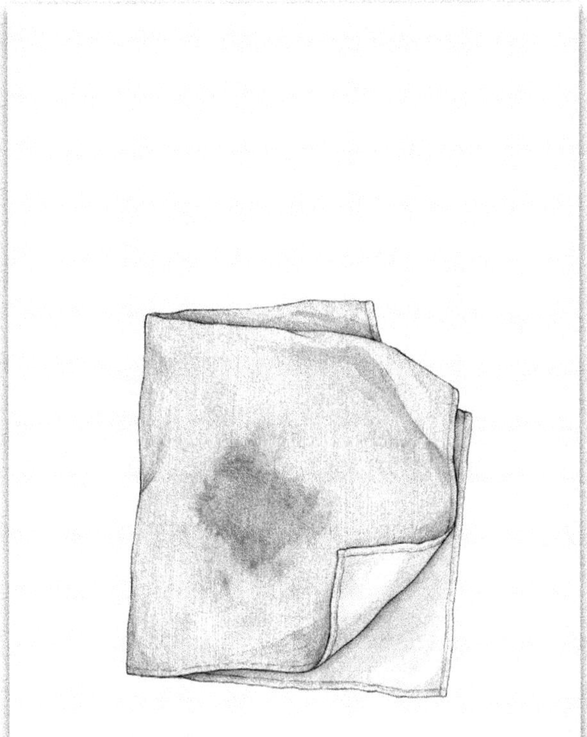

At night the mind still tried to rule.

Loops appeared, familiar and insistent.

I watched them loosen without becoming commands.

Anger still appeared.

But the reflex began to break.

I could hold it without becoming it.

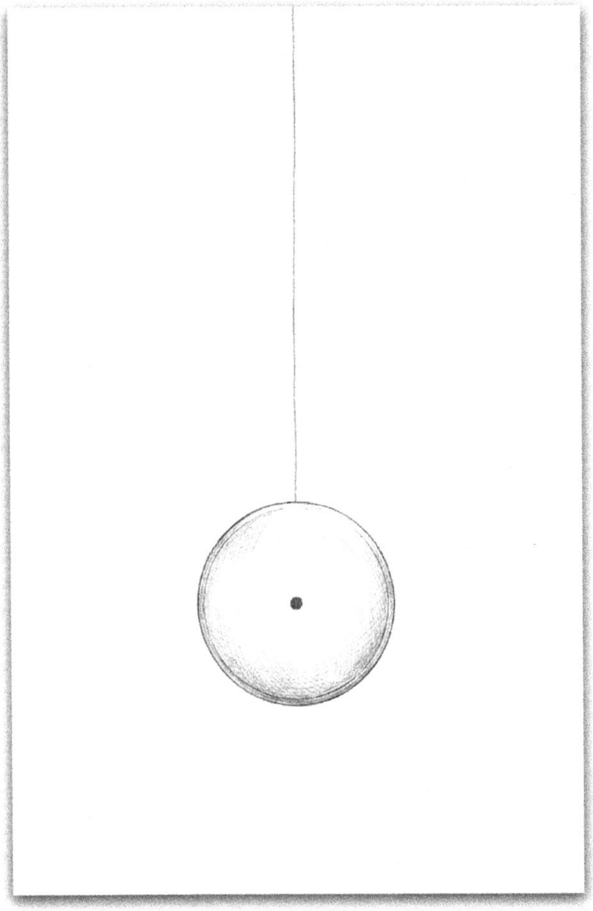

I admitted my capacity for hate.

The admission loosened something knotted.

Warmth returned, small and bodily, without ceremony.

Lower down, things felt unfamiliar.

As if the mind stored old nightmares there.

I went slowly, and did not force entry.

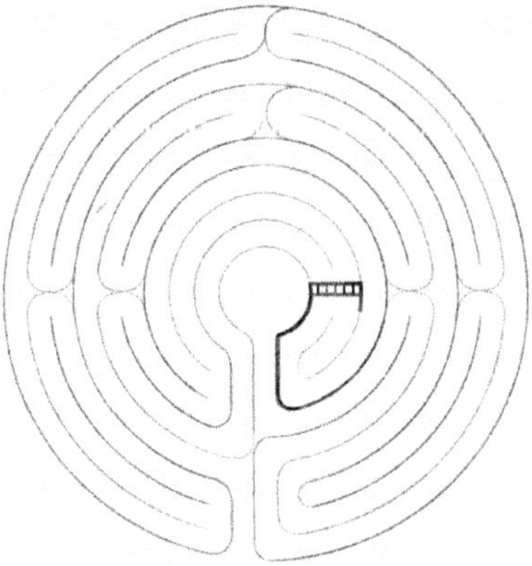

Light reached me with less distortion.

The world didn't hook me the same way.

I felt quieter, less provoked, more intact.

Chapter 7

I stopped expecting change to feel like comfort.

It felt more like heat—careful, contained—then cooling.

Not a rescue, not a sudden lift. A quiet workshop:

nsomething in me being tempered, a little at a time.

I could tell, without being able to prove it, that the darkest phase had loosened.

Not gone—just no longer absolute.

Something like clearing had begun: soot lifting, residue thinning, the same life letting a little more light through.

The old moral labels started to feel blunt.

Not meaningless—just too heavy for what was actually happening.

I watched the mind reach for "good" and "bad" as if it could end the story, and I let those words hang there without obeying them.

I went back down through the layers again and again.

Memory surfaced. Old reactions rose like sediment.

I stayed close to the feeling without feeding it, until it began to lose its charge—until it became "what happened," not "what I am."

Things that used to hook me began to pass through.

Not because they were suddenly acceptable, but because they didn't stick into the same wound.

The barb wasn't finding purchase the way it used to.

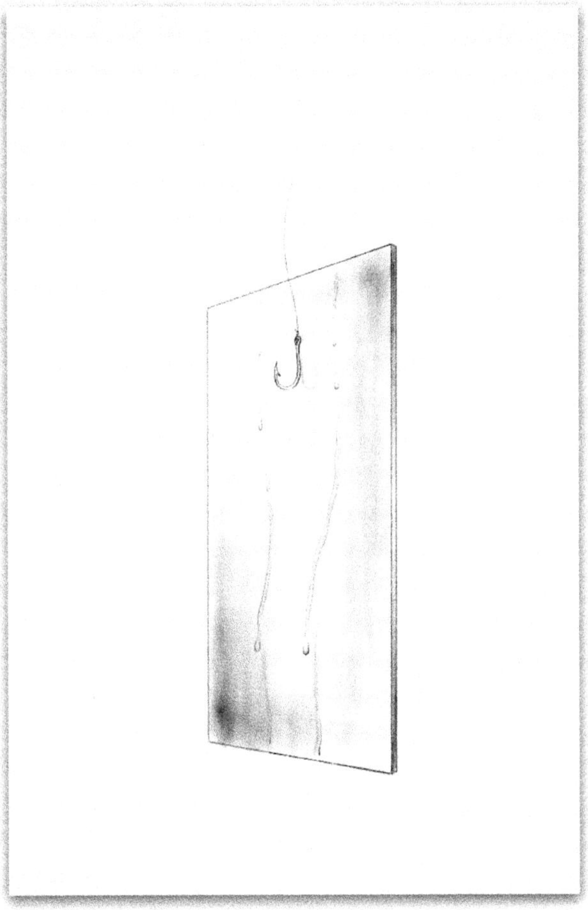

Temptation still appeared, but it stopped feeling like a verdict. More like a pull—directional, persuasive, familiar. I could sense it as "toward," and just as clearly, sense what "away" meant, without turning it into a war.

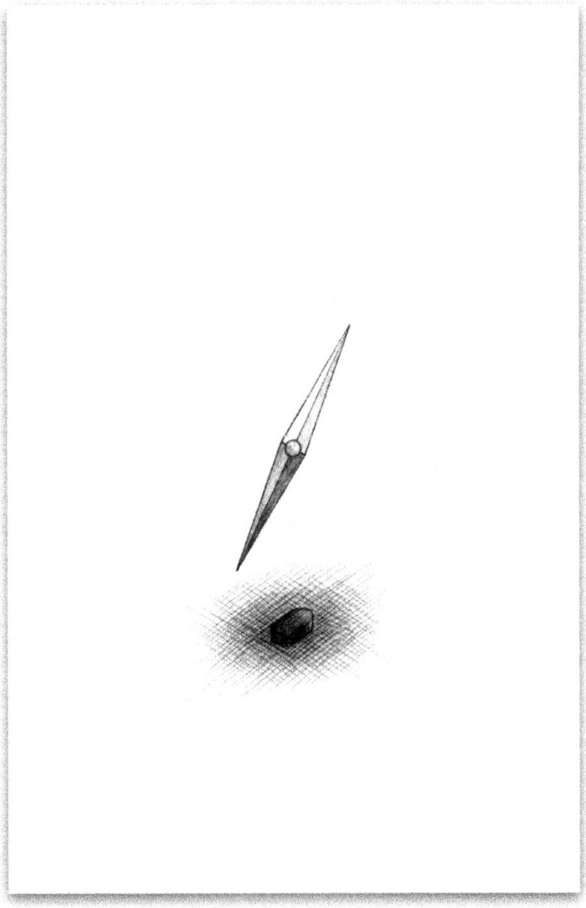

I could admit what was true about me without collapsing.

Not as self-punishment—more like simple accuracy.

When I stopped defending, a strange energy returned: what I'd spent years holding down came back as room to breathe.

Protection began to form inside me rather than around me.

It wasn't numbness. It wasn't a mask.

It felt like a different substance—moral metal, not heavy plating—

something steady that didn't need to threaten anyone.

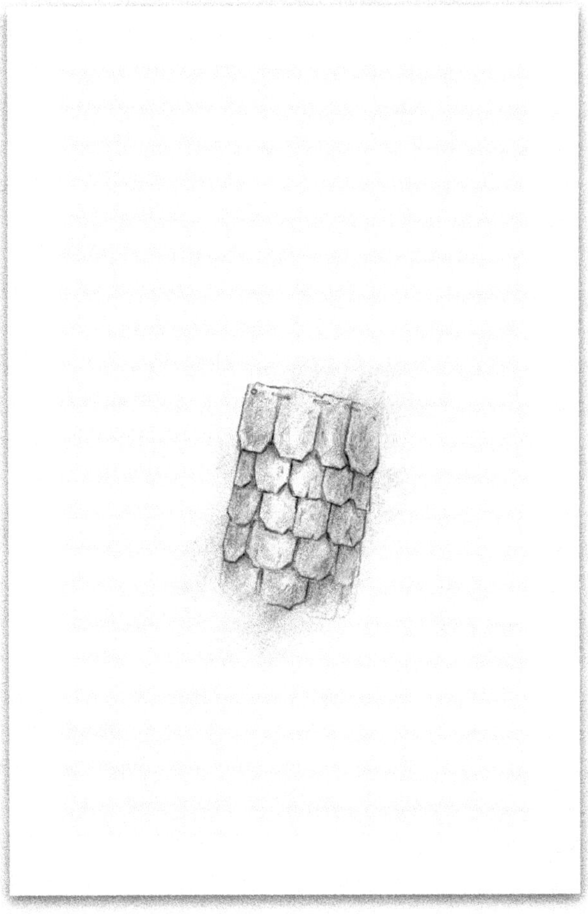

The changes became noticeable—not just to me.

And with that came a new danger: comparison, a private sense of being "ahead," a tightening in the chest that wanted credit.

I recognised it as a fresh distortion, not a reward.

There was a place in me I had avoided.

Not because it was dramatic, but because it was cold—still—sealed.

I approached it slowly, as if coming to the edge of a lake I didn't want to look into.

Betrayal memories surfaced.

Then the harder ones: the moments I left myself behind—small choices, repeated, that I had called "necessary."

The wound wasn't only what others did. It was also the part of me that stopped protecting what mattered.

The fear shifted when I stopped calling it "not me."

Distance collapsed into recognition.

Whatever I had named as enemy was also a part of my own structure —frozen, protective, misdirected—and compassion became possible without approving of harm.

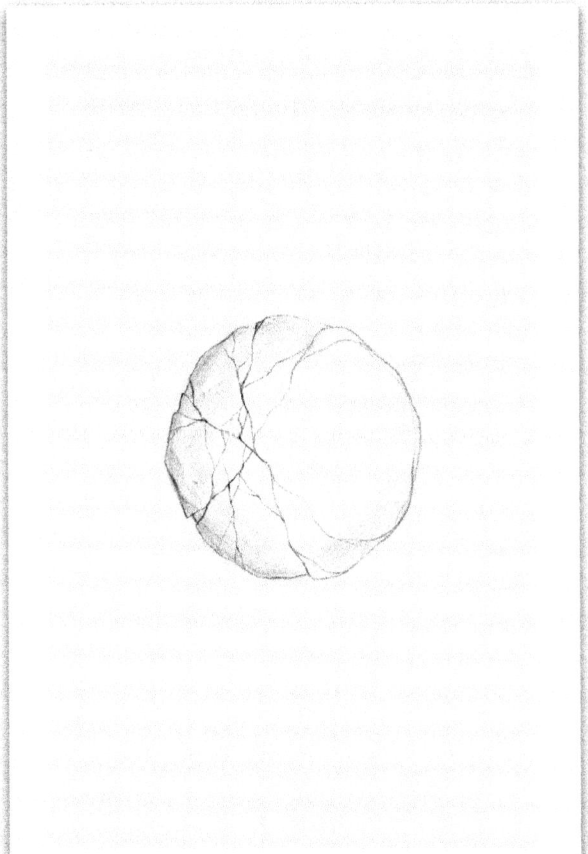

Something in me warmed that I had believed would stay frozen.

Not ecstasy—more like inevitability: ice giving way under steady heat.

A sealed adversary becoming movement again, the old "tempter"

changing shape as light returned to places I had kept unlit.

In the remembered language of symbols, the fallen adversary became a light-bringer again.

Not a coronation. Not a victory.

More like a single upward spiral: the parts rising together, unfinished, with humility required—because the work could still be claimed by pride if I wasn't careful.

Chapter 8

I reached the floor.

Not in a dramatic way—more like a simple fact:

it stopped getting worse.

There was nowhere left to fall,

and that meant I could finally stand without pretending.

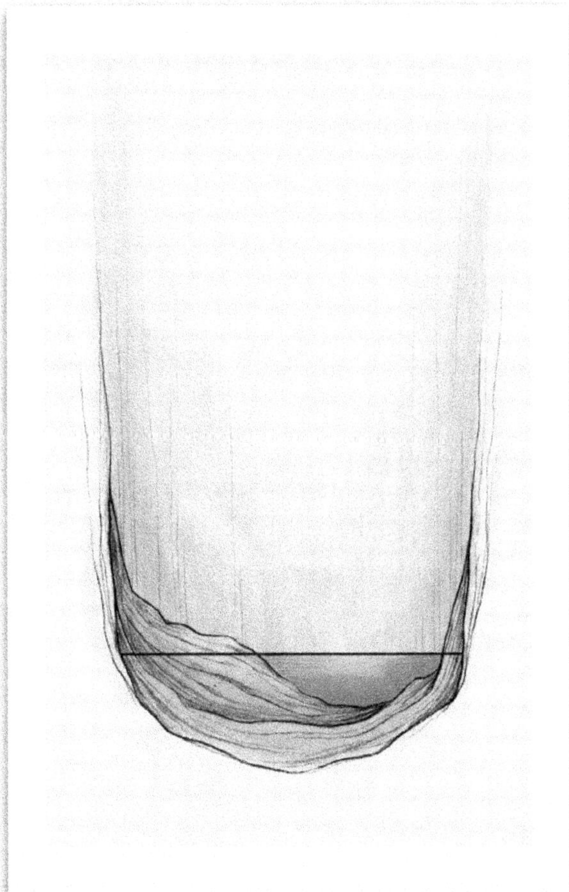

My urge to condemn thinned.

I could see how people move when they're afraid,

or small, or trying to be safe.

Their harm didn't become "good,"

but it stopped becoming the whole story of them.

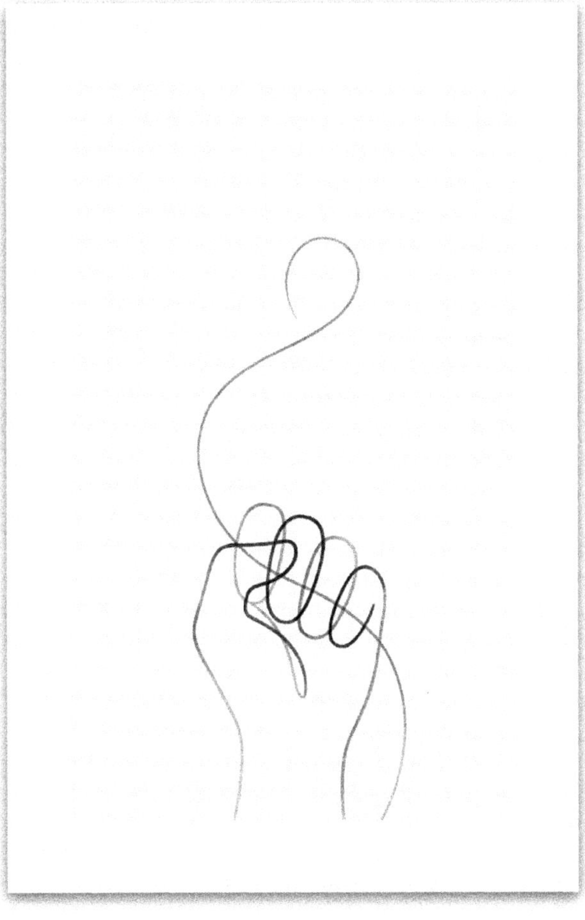

I stopped pretending I was only one thing.

I included what I used to hide—without pride, without theatre.

The darkness didn't vanish; it became acknowledged, and that changed its weight.

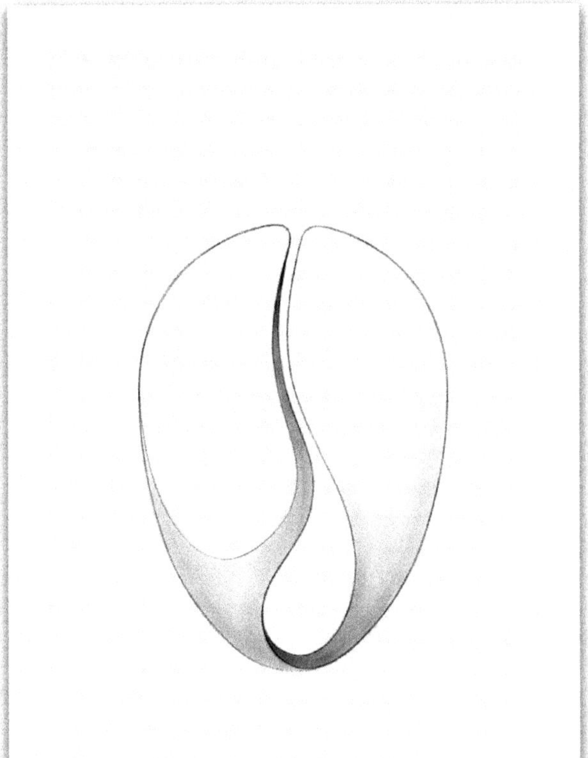

From down here, the world looked unromantic—almost plain.

And somehow that plainness felt honest.

It was like listening from inside a cistern: every echo stripped of performance.

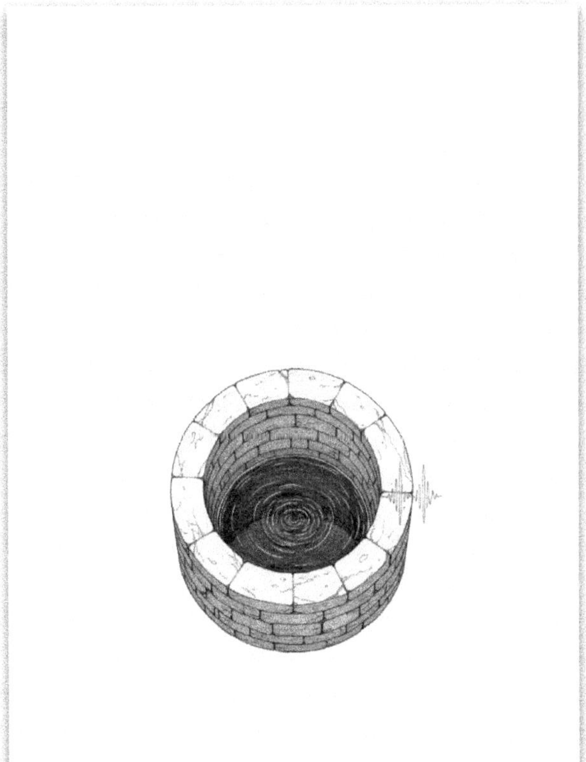

What used to weigh me began to feel like heat with a purpose.

Not pleasant—usable.

A new skin forming: not armour to hide behind, but something tempered that could hold contact.

Strength showed up quietly.

And with it, a tenderness: the sense that something new in me could be damaged easily.

Like a small creature learning its shape—alive, untrained, needing protection from attention.

Old hooks still appeared.

They just didn't pull with the same force.

When something snagged, it felt more like a reminder that residue returns—quietly—and needs time to settle again.

Then pride arrived—fast, chemical.

A flicker of authority I hadn't earned, a hunger for respect that felt dangerous.

It frightened me more than pain, because it could turn the whole process into a new disguise.

I learned to keep the work unnamed.

Not as a secret to feel special—more like shelter.

Some things strengthen best when they aren't explained, defended, or displayed.

I could feel three qualities settling into a workable arrangement:

weight, heat, and a small living centre.

Not a theory—just a tactile sense of alignment that made the day less jagged.

People expected the old responses.

I met them differently, and it felt awkward—like wearing a familiar coat that no longer fit.

I kept compassion quiet, and let ordinary contact be enough.

The moment got louder.

Planning became harder—not because life was solved, but because the future stopped being the only place my mind lived.

It felt like rising through layers: not ascending to victory, just becoming less burdened by what wasn't here.

There were moments—brief, unmistakable—when joy arrived without effort.

Not as a promise, not as permanent proof.

Just a clean ignition: ash-lightness, the body remembering how to feel alive.

I felt the difference between hiding and lying.

When I told the truth—plainly, without weapon—something heavy dropped away.

Integrity didn't make me better than anyone; it made me lighter inside my own skin.

Chapter 9

I grieved a version of myself I could not go back to.

Not a dramatic death—more like a slow recognition that the old competence had gone.

The loss sat in me for a long time, plain and heavy, without a clear place to put it.

Something new began, and it was small.

Raw in a way I didn't want seen, as if attention alone could bruise it.

I held it carefully—not as a secret to elevate me, but as a life that needed shelter.

I found myself borrowing old words—fall, grace, resurrection

—because ordinary language didn't fit.

Not as doctrine.

More as emotional shorthand for something that had ended, and

something that had begun without fanfare.

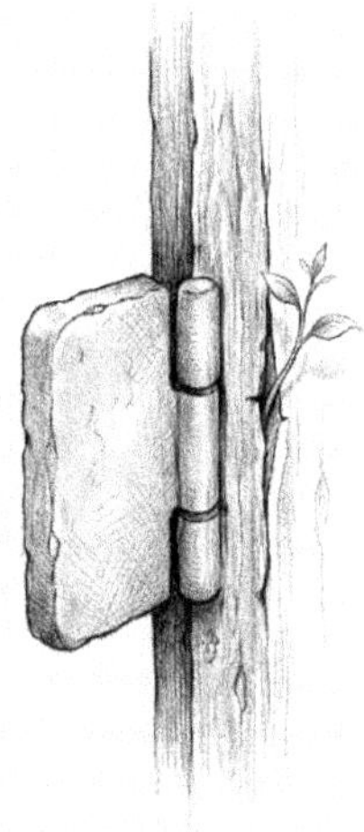

I looked straight at what I had tried not to be.

The animal impulses didn't vanish, but they stopped haunting me when I stopped pretending they were foreign.

They became part of the weather of being alive—something to notice without worshipping or condemning.

Relief arrived, and then excitement surged—too much, too fast.

Joy had an edge to it, like a bright current that could tip into intoxication.

I noticed how easily lightness could become momentum, and momentum could become a problem.

A sweet pull appeared: to be seen, admired, placed above.

It tasted good and immediately wrong.

Not because admiration is evil, but because I could feel how quickly it would turn into a new identity—heavy with authority I hadn't earned.

I noticed familiar currents moving through me like weather.

Heat. Hunger. Comparison. Dullness.

They weren't sins on a tally sheet—just patterns I could feel arriving, passing, and sometimes staying longer than I wanted.

I remembered how much I don't know.

It didn't shame me; it settled me.

Ignorance, held honestly, felt like a steady baseline—proof that I was unfinished, and that unfinished could be safe.

I could still be provoked.

Buttons still existed; sparks still happened.

The difference was seeing the spark earlier—feeling the heat rise before it became a fire I would later have to explain.

The urge to do good rose in me, bright and persuasive.
And I could feel how quickly brightness can harden—how easily idealism becomes a kind of glare.
What mattered was not the story of "rightness," but whether my goodness stayed soft enough to remain human.

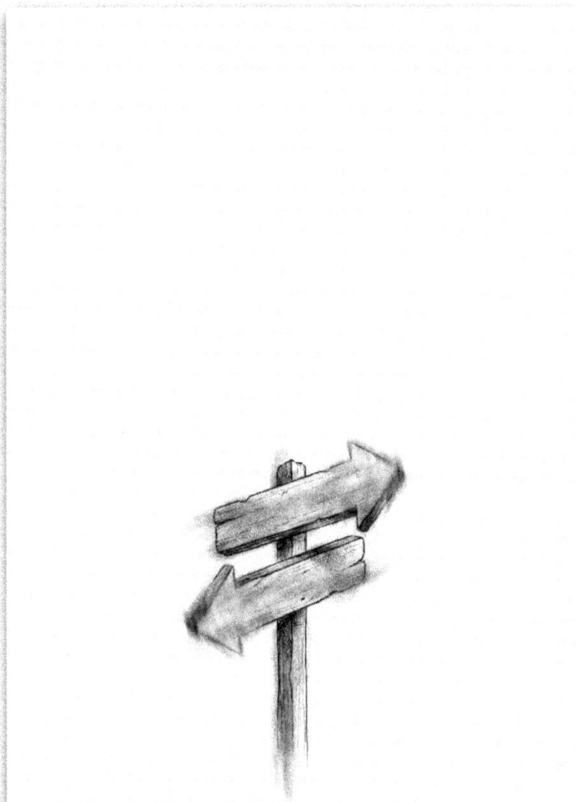

Some days I felt centred in the body—quietly, without effort.

Less craving. Less irritation. Fewer escapes.

Not perfection—just a steadiness that made ordinary life feel less like a negotiation with extremes.

I slipped. I noticed. I returned.

Again and again, without drama.

Centredness wasn't a new identity—it was a repeated return after disturbance, held with curiosity instead of collapse.

Chapter 10

For years I couldn't work.

I watched my days narrow into small tasks and long blanks, and I didn't recognise myself inside it.

The confusion wasn't occasional—it was the air I lived in.

I looked for help and found gaps.

Not cruelty—just a mismatch between what was happening

and the maps I was offered.

That mismatch became its own pain: being named, but not met.

I worked through the day, and studied at night.

Spare time became a lab—notes, books,

and the same questions circling back.

It wasn't ambition. It was pressure: the need to understand

what a mind could do to itself.

I spent hours with images that refused to be straightforward.

The symbols didn't give answers;

they gave resistance—something to sit with.

Over time it felt as if the page was watching me back, not with menace,

but with insistence.

Familiar stories stopped being facts and became mirrors.
I didn't need to believe them in order to recognise myself in them.
The language returned because it could hold the shape of what I felt,
without pinning it down.

I met parts of myself I didn't want to name.

Not as villains—more as abandoned fragments, carrying old heat.

I could feel shame rise, and still I stayed close enough to see what was there.

I stopped trying to be one thing.

Some days I was dim and unfinished. Some days I was hot and reactive.

Some days I was soft and idealistic.

Holding the mixture didn't solve me—it steadied me.

The steadiness came in ordinary moments.

Not when I chased it, and not when I tried to prove I had it.

It arrived quietly—almost like something I noticed after it had already happened.

The less I named it, the cleaner it stayed.

If I spoke too soon, it turned into a story—and the story pulled attention toward me.

Silence wasn't a vow. It was protection.

At times it felt as if something in me was held in place.

Not punished—just fixed, as though movement had paused long enough for a deeper settling.

The image that came was simple geometry: a crossing of lines, a point held.

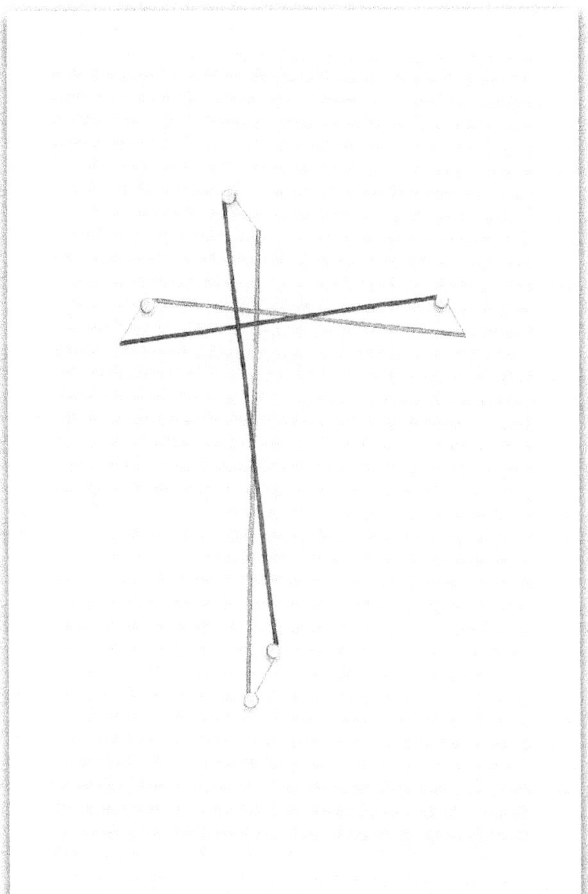

Before words, there was sensation.

Churn low in the belly. Tightness behind the ribs. A catch in the throat.

Meaning came later—sometimes much later—after the body had already spoken.

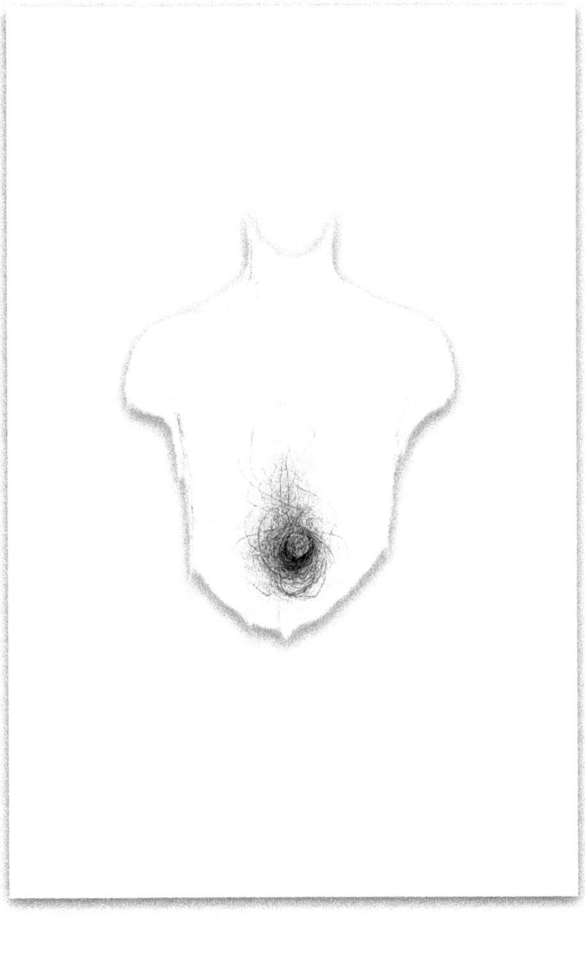

At night, something happened.

In the morning, it was smoke—an aftertaste without a story.

I could sense there had been movement, but the details wouldn't hold.

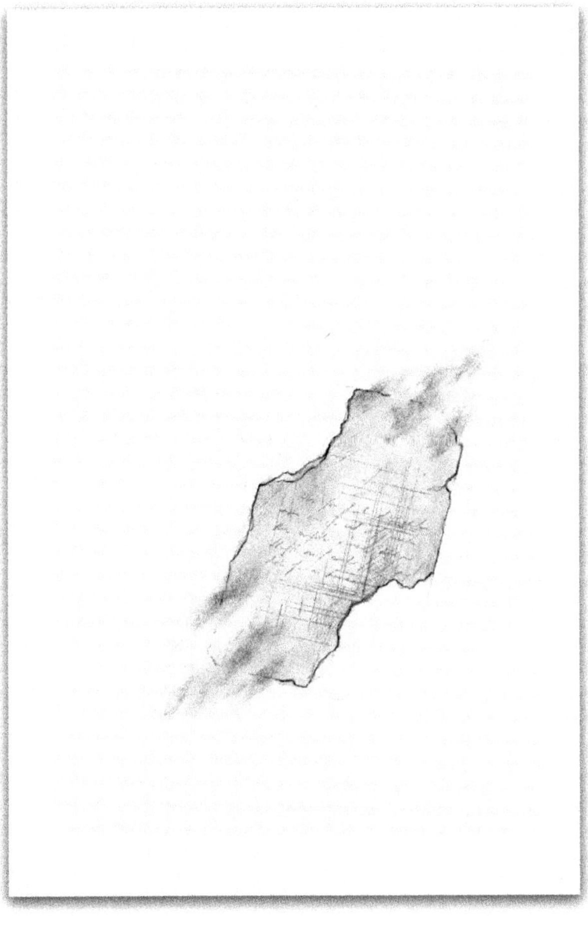

Some parts of me stayed stuck in old alarms.

Not memories like films—more like small locked positions that the body still remembered.

I didn't force them open. I just acknowledged they were there.

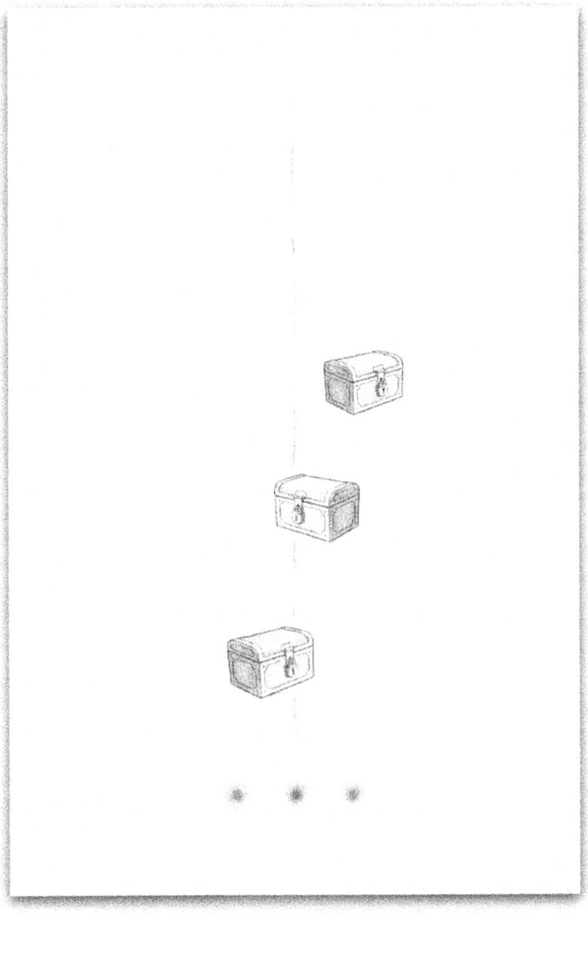

The steadiness began to feel real—then the temptation arrived.

A thought that I was done, that I had something to declare, that I could speak with authority.

That impulse frightened me more than the collapse ever did.

Chapter 11

Joy arrived without permission.

Not earned, not summoned—just present, bright enough to unsettle me. Desire loosened around it, and I didn't know whether to trust the lightness or simply witness it.

The day began to feel as if it was answering me.

Numbers repeated. Phrases returned. Small convergences gathered weight.

I didn't know what to do with the pattern-feeling, and I didn't want to turn it into certainty.

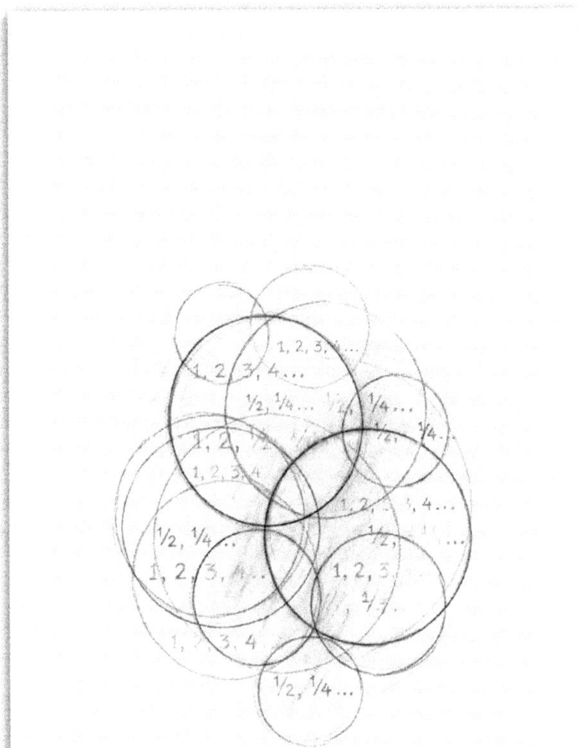
1, 2, 3, 4...
1/2, 1/4...
1, 2, 3, 4...
1/2, 1/4...
1, 2, 3, 4
1/2, 1/4...

Things stood apart, unlabelled.

A cup was simply a cup—stark, crisp, almost too itself.

The usual story around objects went quiet, and what remained felt plain and strange.

Light seemed to come from inside things.

Not as a claim—just as a felt quality of the moment:

points, motes, edges.

The world felt unusually vivid,

and I stayed careful with the word "meaning."

I could enjoy without reaching.

Pleasure came, and the grasping didn't follow.

It felt like a decoupling—attention resting on what was present, without trying to own it.

People projected onto me.

Fear, reverence, suspicion—none of it felt personal,

and all of it felt dangerous.

I could feel how easily a changed presence becomes

a screen for other people's stories.

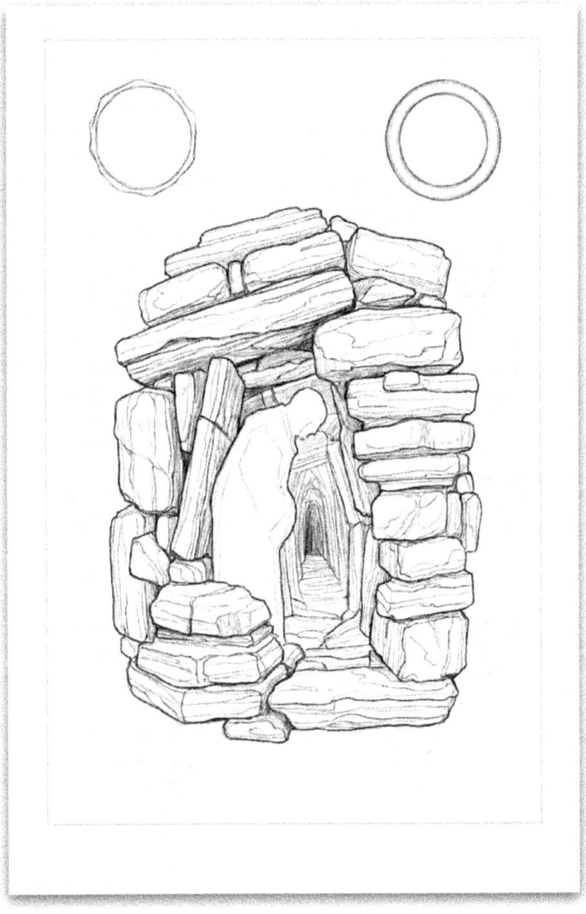

Sometimes I did what felt simple, and later it looked strange.

Not wisdom—just a kind of plainness that didn't fit the usual performance.

I couldn't tell whether it was clarity, awkwardness, or both.

The edge of "me" felt less firm.

Experience moved like a current—sensations arriving and leaving without needing ownership.

It wasn't bliss; it was a thinning of the usual border.

A threshold appeared that didn't accept luggage.

Old identities felt too heavy to carry across.

I didn't force a crossing—

I just saw that some things couldn't come with me.

Attention gathered around me, and I felt the danger of being believed.

The temptation wasn't only mine—it lived in the room,

in the relief people wanted.

I stepped back from any "chosen" story,

because the cost of that story is always harm.

I wrote as if sending letters inward.

Memoir as a kind of contact with lost parts—

then left on the table, unmailed.

Not a message for the world.

A record for what had been separated.

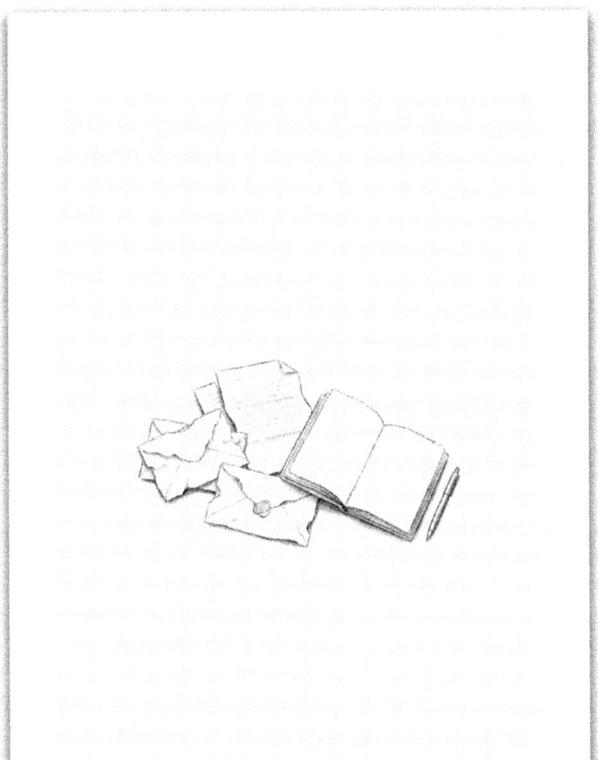

When thought looped back to "me," something tightened. Self-reference felt like friction—attention trying to hold itself. I could feel the discomfort of the loop without turning it into a problem to solve.

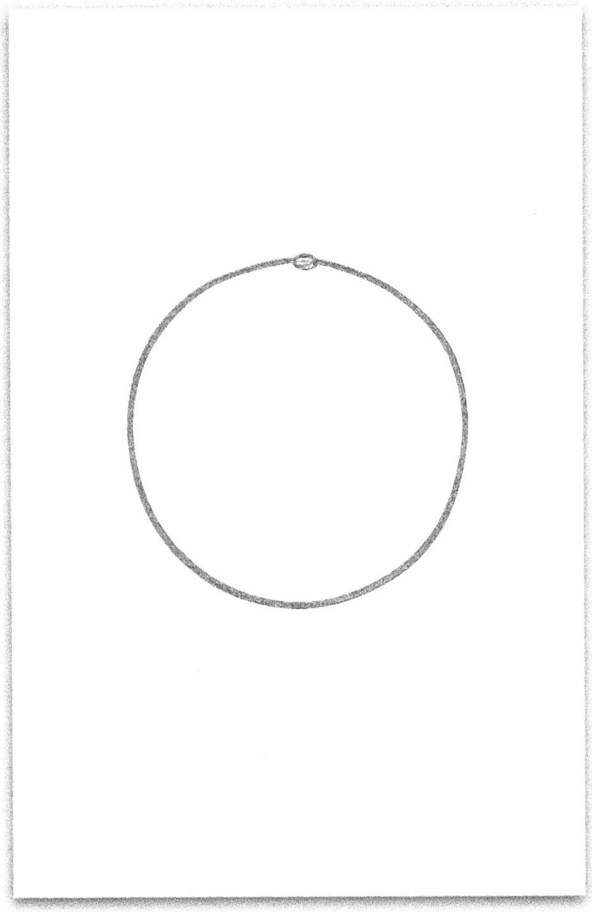

Compassion widened, and with it came a trap:

the urge to reach and fix.

I could feel how saving-impulse flatters the self and harms the other.

So I held the conflict—care without conquest.

The territory became unbelievable,

and the shift kept happening anyway.

I didn't know how to speak about it without damaging it.

So I stayed small inside it, and watched for the places where strain began to show.

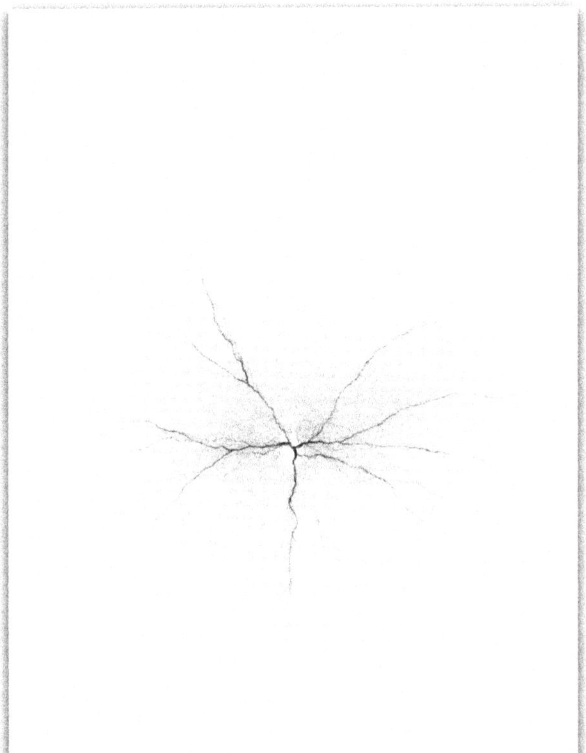

Chapter 12

The journey began as a crisis and became a landscape. Now it feels like the landscape is thinning. Not resolved—just quieter. As if the air has changed, and a door is nearing the end of its swing.

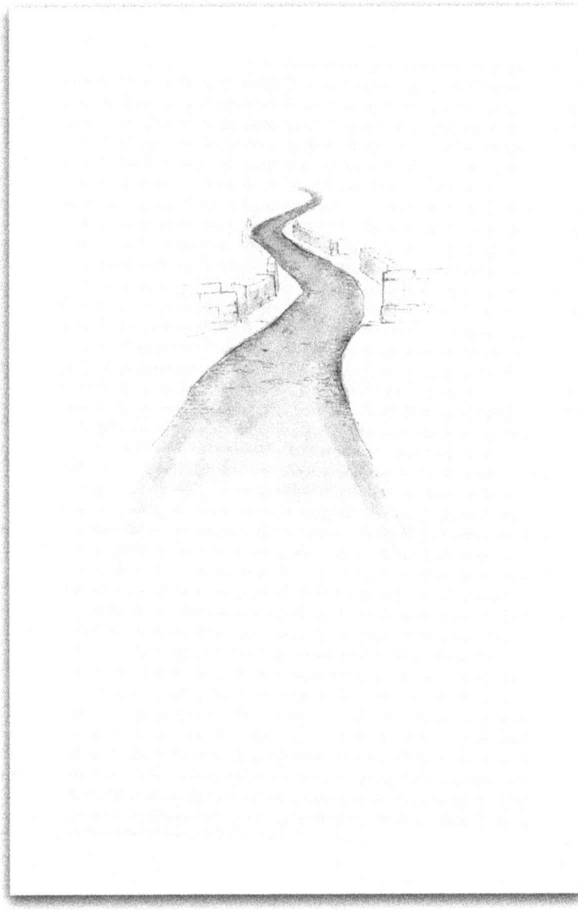

I keep noticing how the same events can be read two ways. One way: an illness that stole years. Another way: a threshold I stumbled across and never fully walked back from. The second reading doesn't comfort me. It just sits there, uninvited, asking to be held without certainty.

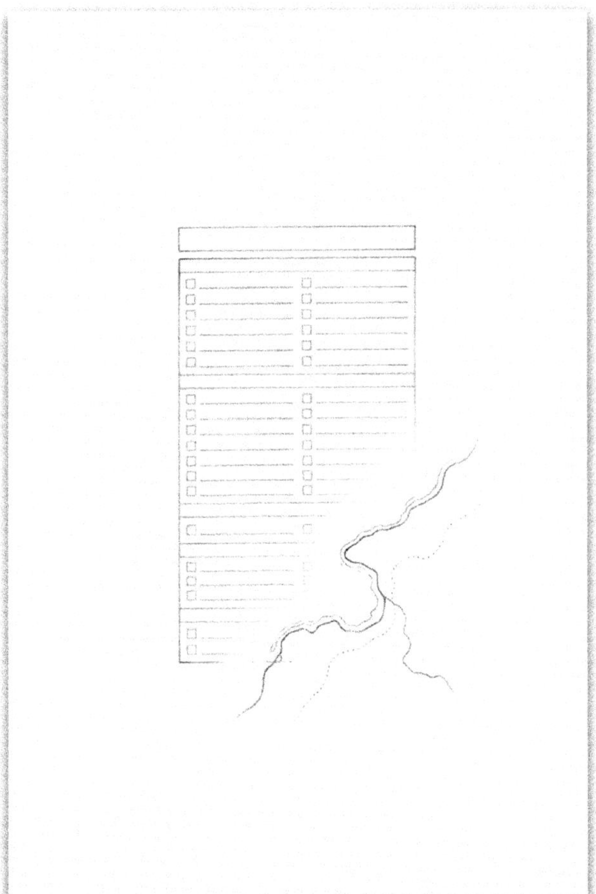

There's a kind of brightness that isn't warmth. It doesn't feel like comfort or joy. It feels like precision—like something clean and hard that language can't grip without smearing. When I try to describe it, the words arrive already wrong.

I don't feel a climax coming. I feel strain. Like a container that has done its job for a long time, quietly, and is now reaching a limit it never agreed to name. The pressure is not loud. It is persistent.

Daylight thinking looks thin from here—useful, functional, but strangely surface-level. I watch it do what it does: label, plan, brace, explain. It isn't wrong. It just isn't the whole of what's happening.

Sometimes it feels like one mouth with several speakers. Hunger speaks. Fear speaks. The old self-protection speaks. Thought narrates after the fact, as if it was there at the beginning. I don't feel like a single unit. I feel like a crowded room trying to use one name.

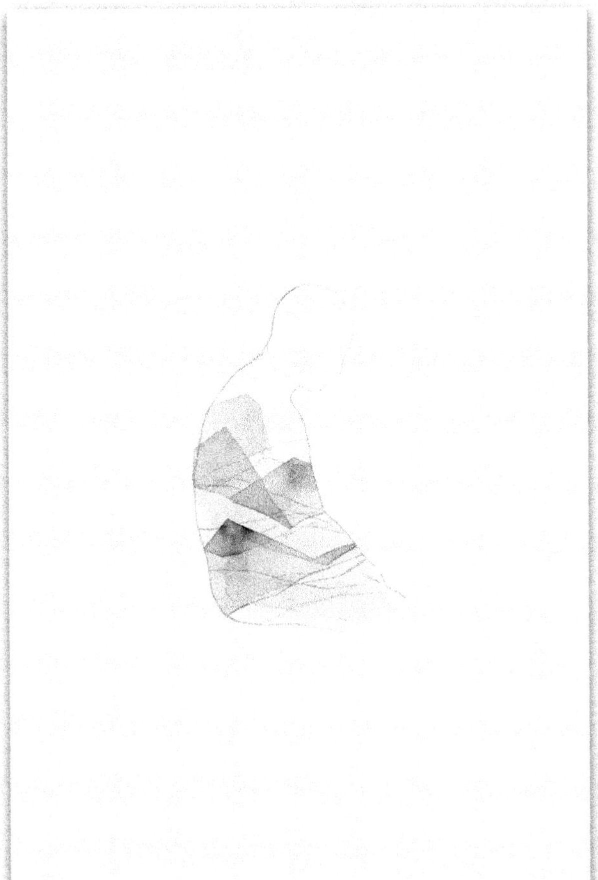

Sensation arrives clean. Then meaning arrives. Then commentary. Then a conclusion I didn't ask for. When I notice the sequence, it's almost embarrassing—how quickly the mind dresses the raw world in its own wardrobe.

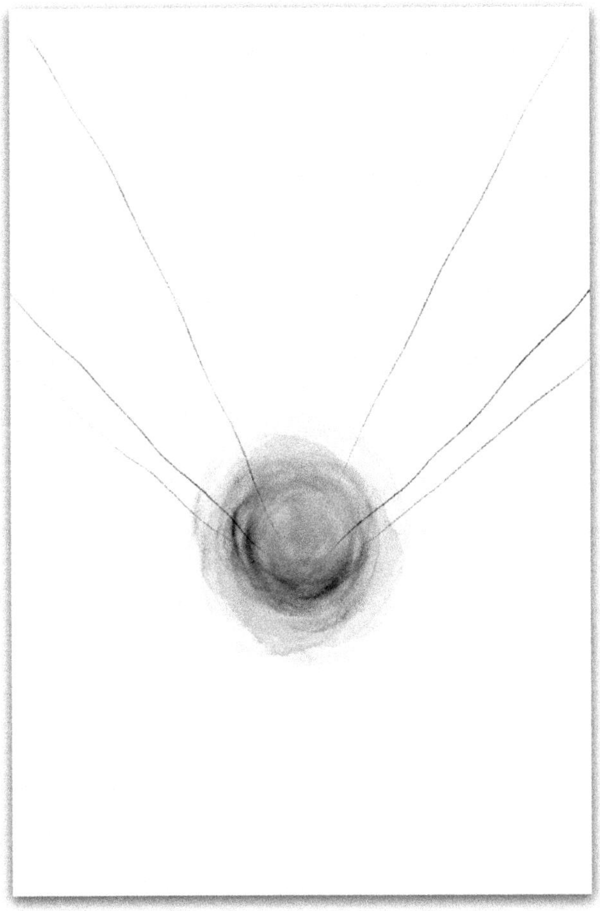

When attention turns back to "me," something tightens. The clarity pinches into a loop. It's like trying to look directly at the act of looking—everything becomes feedback, and the room gets smaller.

I keep scanning for the right shape—an answer, a key, a final word. And the more I search, the more I miss the plainness already present. It's not a lesson. It's just what I keep watching happen.

What I refuse in myself has a way of returning wearing someone else's face. It feels like a trick until I see how consistent it is. The shadow isn't evil. It's simply the part of the story I keep trying to cut out.

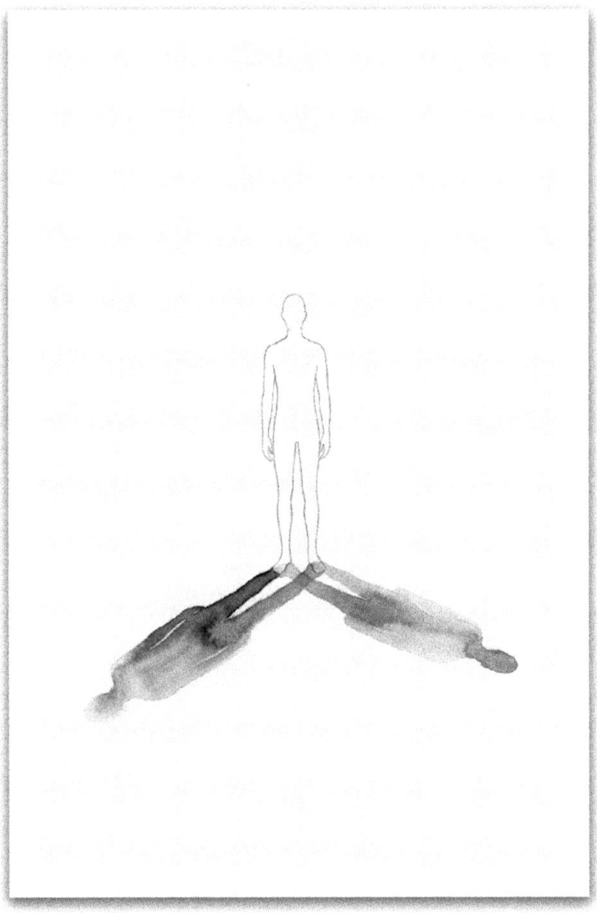

The mind sorts before I notice it sorting. It attaches labels like it's trying to keep the world from moving. I watch the small reflex: yes/ no, safe/ unsafe, mine/ not mine. It doesn't feel malicious. It feels automatic—old machinery still running.

Every description feels like a reflection. Even the best ones. The thing itself stays untouched—like a moon that doesn't need the water to be seen, and doesn't improve when the water becomes calm.

A name sticks. Then judgement grows around it. Then the world splits into pairs—right/wrong, pure/impure, winning/failed. It's astonishing how early the dividing line appears, and how long it takes to notice it was drawn by a small hand.

www.ingramcontent.com/pod-product-compliance
Lightning Source LLC
LaVergne TN
LVHW052112210926
848482LV00025B/553
* 9 7 8 1 0 6 8 4 3 1 0 3 6 *